# dB

# THE VISUAL NOTE TAKING HANDBOOK

Use visual notes to get more out
of lectures, lessons,
presentations and books
50+ visual notes of
inspired learning

dB DYANBURGESS

# Table of Contents

# Introduction

IT WAS THE winter of 2013 and I was listening to the inspiring speeches of presenters at a Professional Speaking Conference in Melbourne.

Unable to keep up with the myriad of thoughts and ideas, I gave up on writing notes and started to draw pictures instead.

At the end of the session, I was surprised to find in front of me, a useful page of notes; just not the written ones I was used to.

I discovered that this more creative form of note taking was just what I needed, particularly when listening to new ideas and complex concepts.

Unaware that others were also embracing this technique, my note taking evolved gradually.

I began carrying a notebook and felt tip pen wherever I went. I paid more attention to my technique. And, more and more often, the visual notes seemed to come to life on the page.

Later, I did an internet search about my new-found interest and it turned out I wasn't alone in my enthusiasm for visual note taking.

At the top of my search was Mike Rohde who champions a style of note taking that he calls 'sketchnoting'. Through his books and blogs, Mike encourages others to share their visual note taking creations via his Sketchnote

Army. He believes passionately that anyone can become a sketchnoter and has certainly helped me to improve my technique and to find my own style.

It's been a fun and rewarding journey, which I would heartily encourage you to take.

# What is a Visual Handbook

THIS HANDBOOK IS a starting point for your own visual note taking journey.

There are many different reasons for taking this journey. For some it will be the enjoyment of drawing and creating. For others it will be the challenge of developing a new skill. And for many it will be a desire to learn and remember more (after all, that's usually the reason we take notes).

Whatever your reason, the good news is that you can start today!

This book is a collection of more that 50 visual notes that I have created over the last few years. They are not about showing you the right way to do visual note taking, but rather to help you with ideas to get you started. I've kept the book nice and compact so you can carry it with you for inspiration, while building your own techniques.

The beautiful thing about this process is that you will develop your own creative tricks and styles; the outcomes are as diverse and complex as our individual brains.

One important point to remember is that there is a difference between art and visual note taking.

Don't become intimidated by note takers who are artists. The main thing is to develop a style that suits you; just engaging in the process of visual note taking will have amazing benefits for your creativity and your ability to learn the content, so relax and enjoy!

When starting out you can simply use the images, shapes, symbols and pictures that you are confortable with (for some people this is essentially letters, numbers, arrows, and shapes, with the occasional star or flower). But you can be guaranteed that this 'toolkit' will gradually grow as you develop your skills (most visual note takers practice drawing specific pictures as they discover gaps in their drawing ability).

There are four steps for you to follow (as eloquently sketched by Veronica Erb, in Mike Rohde's *The Sketchnote Handbook*):

(1) Plan
(2) Capture
(3) Refine
(4) Repeat

I've done an interpretation of Veronica's steps as follows:

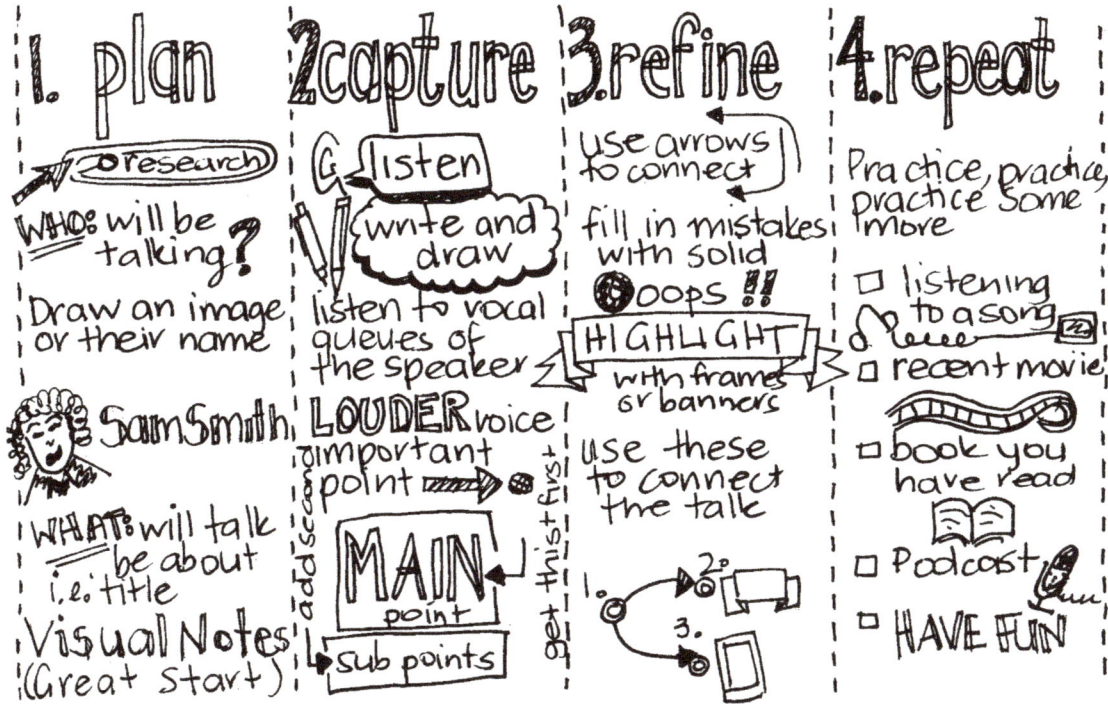

## 1. plan

→ research

WHO: will be talking?

Draw an image or their name

Sam Smith

WHAT: will talk be about i.e. title

Visual Notes (Great start)

## 2 capture

listen

write and draw

listen to vocal queues of the speaker

LOUDER voice

important point →

MAIN point

sub points

add second, get this first

## 3. refine

use arrows to connect

fill in mistakes with solid Ooops !!

HIGHLIGHT with frame or banners

use these to connect the talk

1. 2. 3.

## 4. repeat

Practice, practice, practice some more

☐ listening to a song

☐ recent movie

☐ book you have read

☐ Podcast

☐ HAVE FUN

My spin is slightly different to Veronica's as this is what works for me. You will work out what works for you and create your own version.

So, welcome to the world of visual note taking.

I hope your journey is as enjoyable and educational as mine has been.

Dyan Burgess
April 2016

# Basic Tools

Pen

Pencil

Notebook

Camera or phone (to capture your work and share)

Keen sense of adventure, curiosity and a want to learn (i.e. the right mindset)

**"YOU MUST BE THE CHANGE YOU WANT TO SEE IN THE WORLD.** "

— *Mahatma Gandhi*

# EARLY CHILDHOOD TEACHERS' ASSOCIATION CONFERENCE BRISBANE 2015

**"TEACHERS OPEN THE DOOR, BUT YOU MUST ENTER BY YOURSELF. "**

*— Chinese Proverb*

## Literacy: Practical Ways to Support Young Readers and Writers • Angela Ehmer

**Early Childhood Teachers' Association Conference • Brisbane, 2015**

This fascinating breakout session offered practical techniques to support the different learning styles of young children.

Angela provided real examples and top tips for use in the classroom and beyond.

# The Playful Brain: Development of Young Children's Humour • Dr Paul McGhee

**Early Childhood Teachers' Association Conference • Brisbane, 2015**

The development of humour in young children is an interesting and important topic that many people never think about.

The session was aptly amusing, with hilarious personal stories, as well as broader scenarios.

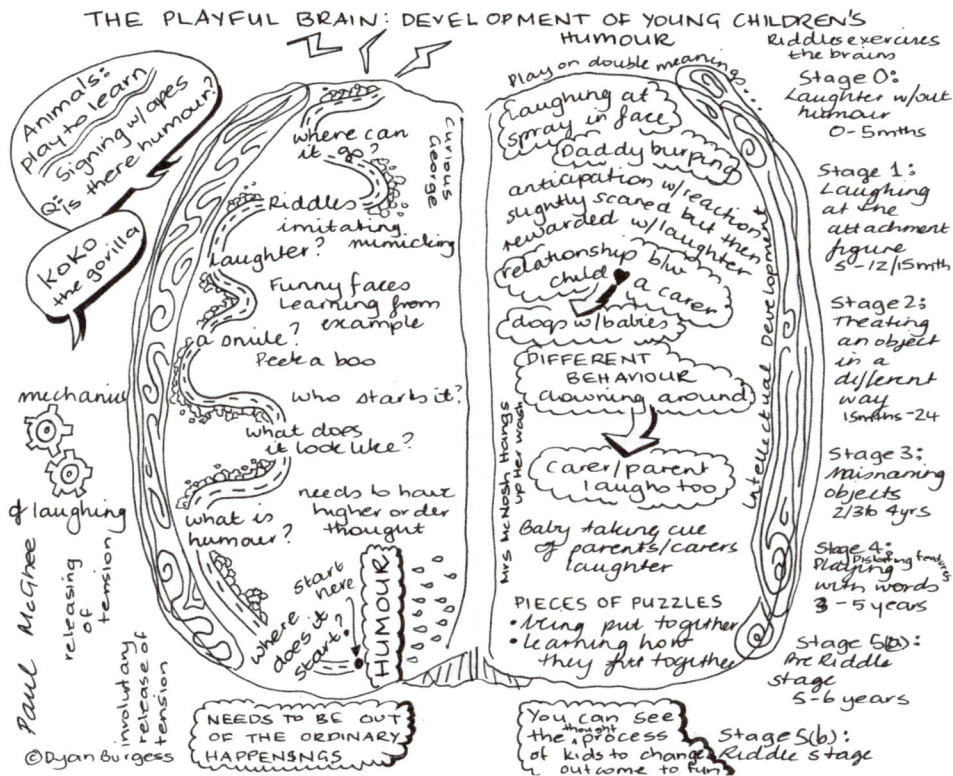

THE PLAYFUL BRAIN: DEVELOPMENT OF YOUNG CHILDREN'S HUMOUR

Animals: play to learn. Signing w/apes. Is there humour?

KOKO the gorilla

Curious George

where can it go?

Riddles imitating. mimicking

Laughter?

Funny faces. Learning from example

a smile?

Peek a boo

mechanical

Who starts it?

What does it look like?

& laughing

what is humour?

needs to have higher order thought

Paul McGhee

releasing of tension

involuntary release of tension

where does it start? start here

HUMOUR

©Dyan Burgess

NEEDS TO BE OUT OF THE ORDINARY HAPPENINGS

Play on double meaning

Laughing at spray in face

Daddy burping

anticipation w/reaction slightly scared but then rewarded w/laughter

relationship blw child & a carer

dogs w/babies

DIFFERENT BEHAVIOUR clowning around

Carer/parent laughs too

Mrs McNosh hangs up her wash

Baby taking cue of parents/carers laughter

PIECES OF PUZZLES
• being put together
• learning how they fit together

You can see the thought process of kids to change outcome to fun

Riddles exercises the brains

**Stage 0:** Laughter w/out humour 0–5mths

**Stage 1:** Laughing at the attachment figure 5–12/15mths

**Stage 2:** Treating an object in a different way 15mths–24

**Stage 3:** Misnaming objects 2/3 to 4yrs

**Stage 4:** Playing with words 3–5 years

**Stage 5(a):** Pre Riddle stage 5–6 years

**Stage 5(b):** Riddle stage

Intellectual Development

**LIGHTEN UP! Humour is FUNdamental to providing Quality Education & Care to Young Children (Keynote) • Dr Paul McGhee**

**Early Childhood Teachers' Association Conference • Brisbane, 2015**

With the focus on humour, it's fitting that there was plenty of laughter during this presentation. And just in case anyone had forgotten how to laugh, Paul tested audience members on their ability to create laughter via a five-step process.

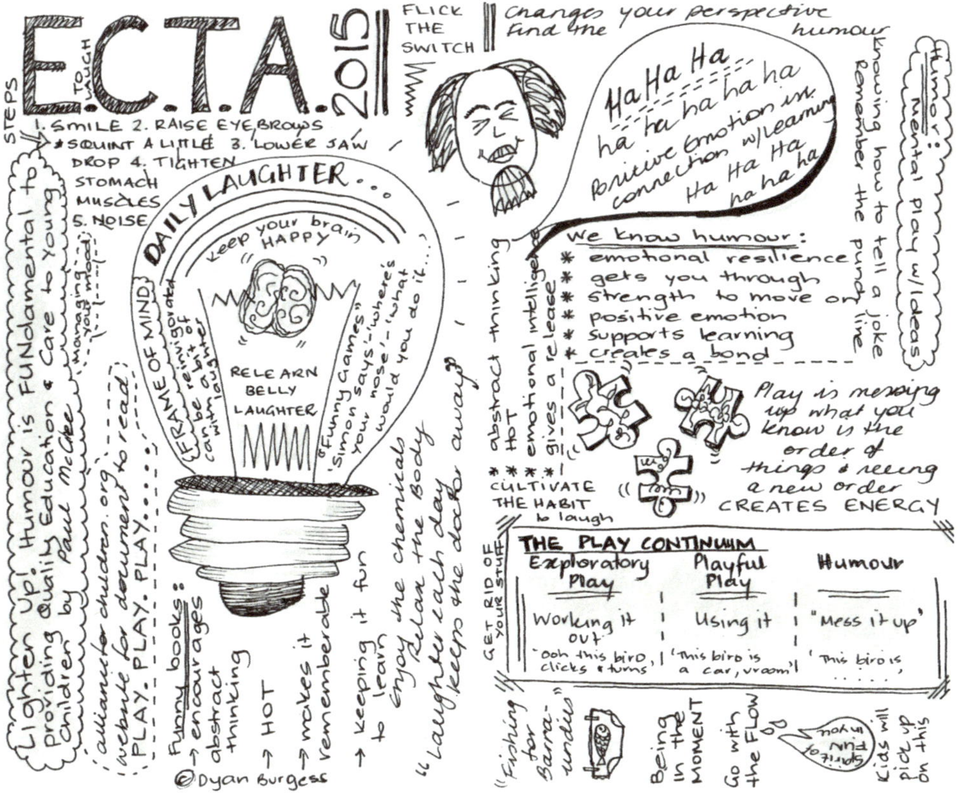

*[Handwritten sketchnote annotations surround the page, including:]*

Lighten Up! Humour is FUNdamental to providing Quality Education & Care to Young Children by Paul McGhee

@dyanburgess

PLAY. PLAY. PLAY...

Funny books: encourages abstract thinking → HOT → makes it remembered → keeping it fun → Relax the body → Enjoy the chemicals → "Laughter each day keeps the docs away?"

THE PLAY CONTINUUM — Exploratory Play / Playful Play / Humour

Working it out / Using it / "Mess it up"

Get rid of your stuff

CULTIVATE THE HABIT to laugh

CREATES ENERGY — a new order, a new thing of order in the chaos

Play is moving up what you know into a new order — gives a release, HOT emotional intelligence, abstract thinking

positive emotion supports learning, strength to move on, emotional resilience gets you through — creates a bond

We know humour: knowing how to tell a joke, remember the punch line

Humor: Mental Play w/ideas, changes your perspective, humour

Flick the switch

FRAME OF MIND — "Funny games" "Simon says — where would you do it" — RELEARN BELLY LAUGHTER — keep your brain HAPPY

DAILY LAUGHTER...

Steps: 1. Smile 2. Raise eyebrows 3. Lower jaw 4. Tighten/Squint a little — TOUGH — Tighten stomach muscles, S. Noise

Ha Ha Ha ha ha ha — balance emotion when learning — Ha Ha Ha

Spirit of FUN in you — Kids will pick up on this

Being in the MOMENT — Go with the FLOW

Funny for bare-undies...

# FOUNDING MUM'S MEET UP

# "TO EARN MORE YOU MUST LEARN MORE." "

— *Brian Tracey*

## Be all you can be … • Anne Aleckson

**Founding Mums' Meetup •
Brisbane, 2015**

What is better: being happy or being right? To move forward, we sometimes need to put aside being right and consider our happiness.

Anne discussed the importance of choosing your happiness and creating the right reality for you. First step is to sort yourself and your self-care; then you can reach new levels of greatness in your life.

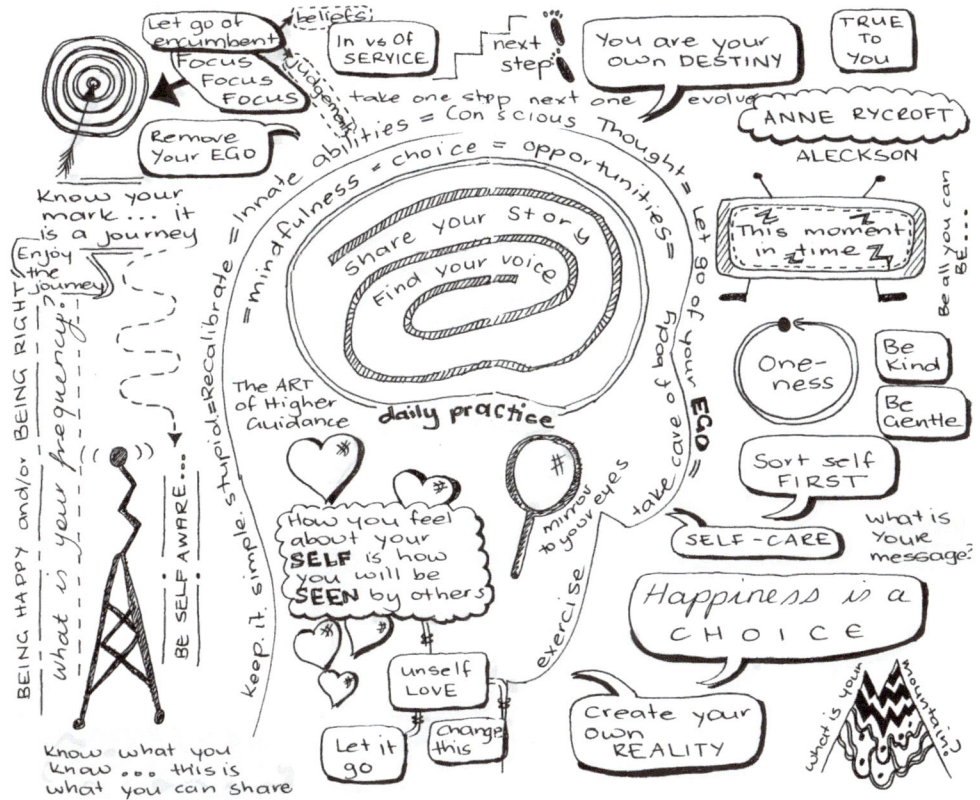

JOHN FLUTTER DENTAL

**dB**

"**THE SUREST WAY NOT TO FAIL IS TO DETERMINE TO SUCCEED.** "

— *Richard B. Sheridan*

## Breathing Program for Straighter Teeth • Kylie

**John Flutter Dental • Brisbane, 2015**

On day one Kylie introduced us to the interesting concept of creating straighter teeth using a whole-body technique.

She particularly focused on posture and the art of breathing through your nose with your lips together.

13 APRIL 2015
**90 days**
13 JULY 2015
Start with *Correct posture*

with Kylie

Breathing Program – JF Dental 13, 14, 15, 16 APRIL

DAY 1

Eyes straight
chest up + forward
back off chair

hands on legs
shoulders down + back
feet flat on floor

Breathe thru' nose
lips together

40 $ETCO_2$

10-12 bpm    TARGET

Shhhh quiet breath

Shoulders still
In + out nose {quiet}

STILL

Create new habits

Build synapses

Walk – hold breath
3 REPS

Exercise with tape on your lips while using muscles
5 minutes

Test your breathing
5 minutes

**PRACTICE**
**3 sets** @ home overnight
tape on @ night with MYO brace

## Breathing Program for Straighter Teeth • Kylie

**John Flutter Dental • Brisbane, 2015**

On day two Kylie took us into deeper understanding and discussion about how to achieve still and silent breathing.

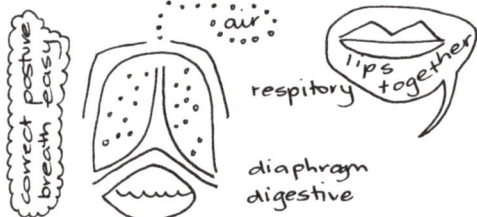

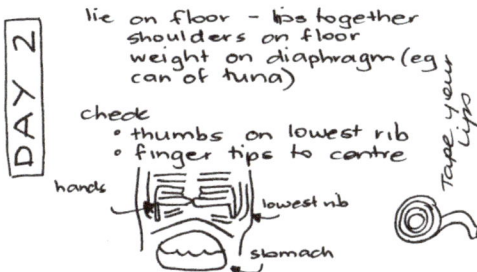

air

correct posture breath easy

respiratory

lips together

diaphragm
digestive

PACE IT OUT

BOUNCE IT OUT

$CO_2$

5 mins
5:00

feet flat
on the floor

**DAY 2**

lie on floor - lips together
shoulders on floor
weight on diaphragm (eg
can of tuna)

check
• thumbs on lowest rib
• finger tips to centre

hands

lowest rib

stomach

Tape your lips

...Then follow the ball breathing

D O W N L O A D

Bouncing Ball Program

**3** SETS   HOME WORK

*Still and Silent Breathing*

lips together
quiet
focused

Keep
feather
still

out   out

breathing with the ball

## Breathing Program for Straighter Teeth • Kylie

**John Flutter Dental • Brisbane, 2015**

On day three Kylie recapped what we had already learnt and checked on our progress to better health.

INHOUSE PUBLISHING

**WORK. FINISH. PUBLISH.**

— *Faradays*

## Self-Publishing Success • Ocean Reeve

### Book summary • 2015

Ocean's book leads you on a step-by-step journey towards self-publishing success.

On the topic of marketing, he presents *The Ten Towers of Triumph* and highlights the importance of each of these in creating your brand.

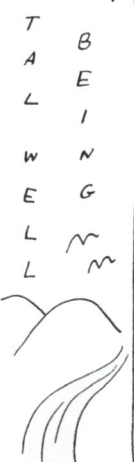
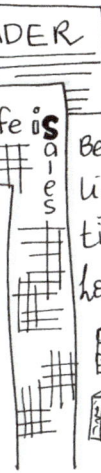

10 TOWERS OF TRIUMPH

OCEAN REEVE: Self-Publishing Success
THE WORD
Book Review

TIMED

TOTAL WELL BEING

Relationships

Achieve your Goals

FINIS

START

PERSONAL DEVELOPMENT

LEADER

Life is Sales

com mun ica tio n...

Be a life time learner

Legacy

key message : You do the best you can with what you know & have available to you & leveraging from that

Features : Hints & tips to leverage off your ownabilities, checklists to get projects off the ground

Key Benefits : enriched experience for you & your children

Emotional : joy, fun, higher response order thinking

Other : Solution to a problem - entertaining children by teaching them to entertain themselves

## Independent Publishing 101 • Ocean Reeve

**InHouse Publishing • Brisbane , 2015**

Ocean outlines a process for producing a trade-standard independently published book.

In particular, he highlights the benefits of the support group associated with the independent publishing industry, as opposed to self-publishing where you are really by yourself.

Attitude, focus and daily hard work are his key ingredients for success.

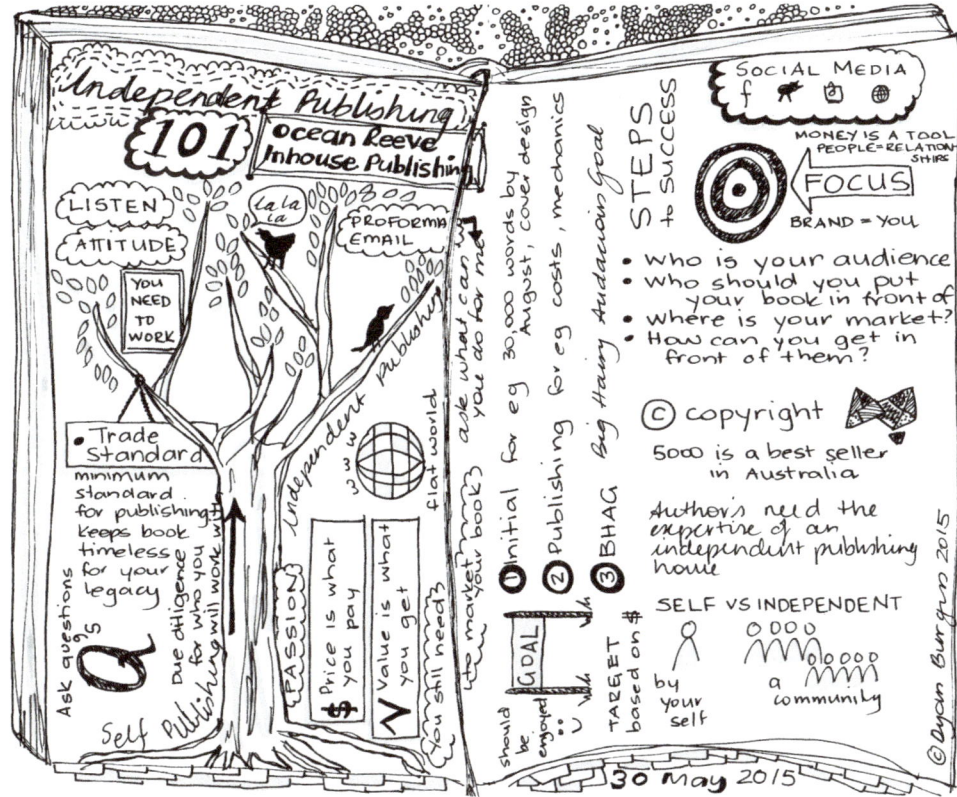

## What it takes to be successful • Dianne Karlsson

**InHouse Publishing Author Day • Brisbane , 2015**

Dianne urges us to step outside our comfort zone and have a leap of faith. Take a Big Step and see where it leads you!

The team at InHouse have a culture based on learning, passion, using humour to cope with stress, getting the job done, and supporting each other.

## The Cranky Guru • Paul Bennett

**InHouse Publishing Author Day • Brisbane , 2015**

Paul calls upon us to act 'as if'; to take a brave leap and be confident that a net will appear.

He discusses the core principles of metaphysics to emphasize how our reality is shaped by our ideas about time, our thoughts, and our beliefs.

# KEY PERSON
# OF INFLUENCE

> **BEFORE YOU ARE A LEADER, SUCCESS IS ALL ABOUT GROWING YOURSELF. WHEN YOU BECOME A LEADER, SUCCESS IS ALL ABOUT GROWING OTHERS.**
>
> — *Jack Welch*

## Five Steps • Glen Carlson

### Key Person of Influence • Brisbane, 2015

Glen outlines the Key Person of Influence program and a five-step process to accelerate your brand.

You need to know what you are known for. By being known for something unique you essentially remove competition.

K.P.I.

KEY PERSON of INFLUENCE

40wks — Flagship program

apply here

[5 STEP PROCESS]

Brand Accelerator

WHAT AM I KNOWN FOR??

Think about this

Connecting
Connectedness
Connect
Connection

Mmmmm

INFLUENCE: Ability to have an affect

5 STEPS:
1. Perfect Pitch
   MATTHEW MICHALEWICZ
2. Building Credibility through Print
   ANDREW GRIFFITHS
3. Productise Your Services
   TIM DWYER
4. Raise Your Profile
   VALERIE KHOO
5. Partnerships & JV's
   MATTHEW MICHAELEWICZ

COMPETITION IS THE ENEMY OF PROFIT

How do I show up in the world to make the competition irrelevant?

# Perfect Pitch • Matthew Michalewicz

## Key Person of Influence • Brisbane , 2015

Step one is about getting the perfect pitch. You need to clearly understand what you can offer, and be able to freely articulate what you do.

After all, it's not necessarily the best service or product that wins; it's the best pitch.

## Content Creation and Book Publishing • Andrew Griffiths

### Key Person of Influence • Brisbane , 2015

Sometimes the key to succeeding is to understand why others fail.

Andrew outlines what has worked for him, as well as the key reasons that people don't publish or books don't do well.

He reminds us that a book is basically a business card on steroids.

(2) BUILDING CREDIBILITY THROUGH PRINT/WRITING

Getting your thoughts out there and defining yourself....

If you are a commodity then only difference is $ price

Publishing House

Content has $ become currency

* I knew my market really well
* I knew what caused them pain - anecdotes
* Practical examples
* Practical tips
* Write how you talk

leveraging power of content

$ Bazingq moments

unique to you

step by step building

opportunity magnet

opening doors

• desire to help others
• shows discipline
• shares value
• conviction
BLOG PODCAST WEBINARS

✝ positive influence

# Productise Your Services • Tim Dwyer

### Key Person of Influence • Brisbane , 2015

Tim outlines a process to productise our services.

We need to understand our product by asking questions such as:

(1)   what is the asset inside us?

(2)   what comes easily to us?

(3)   what problem can we solve?

(4)   what is our core skill set?

His advice includes 'Have fear, but be fearless'.

# NATIONAL SPEAKERS ASSOCIATION OF AUSTRALIA – CHAPTER MEETINGS

**" A LEADER IS A DEALER IN HOPE. "**

— *Napoleon Bonaparte*

## Perfect Prospect Pipeline & Webinar Selling Crash Course • Taki Moore

**National Speakers Association of Australia • Brisbane, 2015**

Taki offers plenty of tips for hosting a fantastic webinar, as well as how to avoid pitfalls and 'not hot' experiences.

Key takeaways include: deliver it forwards, plan it backwards; keep it to three ideas; and know your hook.

N.S.A.A. 11 JUNE 2015

BOOK IN THEIR OWN TIME

where is your – "are you tall enough for this ride?"

① Indoctrination webinar or speech
EVENT
tell us about it
what is this in for me

② Funnel FILTER
WIIFM
self screen in ok out
does this fit for the client ... for you

③ Triage call
do we match if not
see you later. if yes welcome. final check

④ Strategy session
the contact
and let's work together

HOOK
clear if this is for you or if this is not for you

MISTAKES:
1. No opening "are you ..."
2. Teaching too much
   ↳ give the right kind of value
   ↳ Information vs. Transformation
3. Resistible offers
   ↳ needs to be very clear
   ↳ "CLICK HERE NOW"
4. No Stick strategy
   ↳ can you remind me in the QUA's for the link
5. Awkward transition AND Teach then Sell
6. Stopping at the END ↳ Hang about & questions. THE PARTY

Attention Permission to be yourself
Connection
Retention start 5 mins before get the audience ready
HOOK Audience will click
• where are you
• what is the weather
• will show what is the top 3
• just who and what
• webinar

---

### Taki MOORE: Perfect prospect Pipeline & webinar Selling Crash COURSE

#NSAA  #Professionalspeakers
things NOT HOT in webinar – too text heavy
technical difficulties, too pitchy, unclear in purpose

opening / stick / stretch / transition / offer / party

riding the wave
~1.5-2k good range
warm up warm down

PROCESS
SIX STEPS
OPENING  STRETCH
STRETCH TEMPLATE
TRANSITION
CLOSE/OFFER

45 · 10 · 35 ·
Time for 3 things

3 IDEAS

:DELIVER IT FORWARDS: PLAN IT BACKWARDS:

GOOD STUFF:
1. No travel  2. Can be easy (provides value
3. Leveraged selling  4. Value is created in the freespace  5. Set up calendar

# Firing the Mind for Content •
# Allan Parker

### National Speakers Association of Australia • Brisbane, 2014

Allan's twelve techniques to better engage your audience include experimentation, mirroring, creating conversations, and allowing time for questions.

He included practical workshops to demonstrate the techniques and to help listeners fully understand the processes.

## Brand Storytelling Through Video • Michael Hanson

**National Speakers Association of Australia • Brisbane , 2015**

Michael is an expert in creating true storytelling videos.

He highlights the importance of addressing the four 'P's: purpose; people; place; and plot.

Most importantly, you need to understand what drives the person behind the story.

# NATIONAL SPEAKERS ASSOCIATION OF AUSTRALIA – CONFERENCE

**"THE WAY TO WIN IS TO WORK, WORK, WORK, WORK, AND HOPE TO HAVE A FEW INSIGHTS."**

*— Charles T. Munger*

## Anatomy of a Different Kind of Keynote • Steve Simpson

**National Speakers Association of Australia • Canberra, 2015**

Steve dissects the anatomy of a keynote and what it takes to make a great keynote speech.

Congruence is essential. It is also important to be yourself, know your audience and stick to what you know well.

Can you provide the audience with a wonderful journey that they don't want to end?

## Strategy • Lieutenant General David Morrison

### National Speaker's Association of Australia • Canberra, 2015

Is strategy an art or science? According to the dictionary definition, it can be either.

How we develop strategies will depend on our own beliefs about how best to get from point A to point B, but one thing that all strategies need is adaptability.

# How to Stay Fresh, Relevant and Booked Solid • Michael McQueen

## National Speaker's Association of Australia • Canberra, 2015

Staying relevant on the speaking circuit can be challenging.

Michael offers some key questions to help speakers stay focused and fresh:

(1)    what business am I really in?

(2)    what are my non-negotiables?

(3)    what is my unique flavour?

Sometimes you will have to take off the old shoes and try on some new ones.

# Voice is a Choice • Dr Louise Mahler

## National Speaker's Association of Australia • Canberra, 2015

Understanding that your 'voice is a choice' allows you to use your body as an instrument.

By combining your voice, mind and body, you can find your vocal intelligence.

And by making conscious decisions about how you sit and stand, you can develop positive habits for producing your best voice.

## Fit, Fast and Focused • Jenny Brockis

### National Speaker's Association of Australia • Canberra, 2015

By being mindful, you can create positive habits, boost your synapses and utilise your 'lack of finking space'.

Positive daily habits can include refuelling smart, 20-30 minutes of exercise, breaking your day into intervals, and taking time to still your mind or focus on someone else.

## Digital Nomad • Travis Bell

**National Speaker's Association of Australia • Canberra, 2015**

With the mobility of the digital age, there is now a movement of 'digital nomads'.

The Internet of Things (IoT) has allowed us to connect with others who share our passions and to build up a tribe.

However, it is still important to plan your day to ensure you meet and achieve your goals.

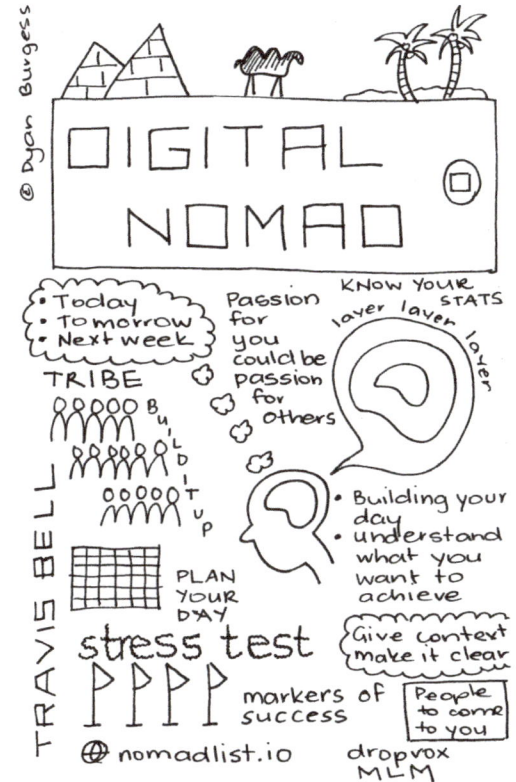

## Achieving Peak Performance • Matthew Favier

**National Speaker's Association of Australia • Canberra, 2015**

Key ingredients for achieving peak performance include: planning and preparation; vision; selecting the right team; daily renewal; and discipline.

Although the ultimate responsibility to achieve our own goals remains with us, it often takes a team effort to achieve success even for an individual. Team support can be especially helpful in clarifying and achieving goals sooner.

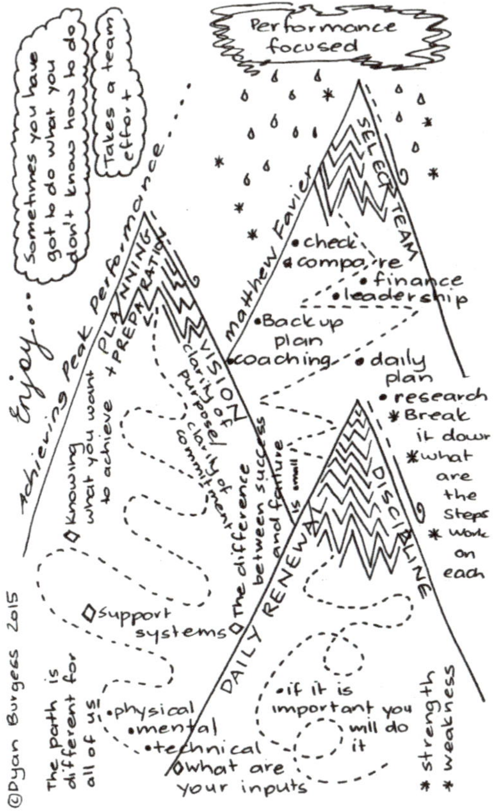

*Handwritten diagram (mind map):*

©Dyan Burgess 2015

- The path is different for all of us
- *strength *weakness
- your inputs
- ◇What are technical, mental, physical
- *it it is important what you will do
- DAILY RENEWALS
- ◇support systems
- the difference between success and failure
- ◇knowing what you want to achieve
- DISCIPLINE
- ⑥ steps are what on each, *what it down, *Break it down, *research
- *daily plan
- VISION
- PLANNING + PREPARATION
- •Back up plan •daily coaching •leadership •finance •compete •check
- SELECT TEAM
- Performance focused
- Sometimes you have got to do what you don't know how to do
- Takes a team effort
- Enjoy... Achieving peak performance

# Tips from the Trenches • Chapter Presidents for each state and territory

## National Speaker's Association of Australia • Canberra, 2015

Tips for succeeding as a speaker include: know when you are hot; let go of self-doubt; and believe in your message.

Define your niche and focus on it. Then go out there and share your content with the world.

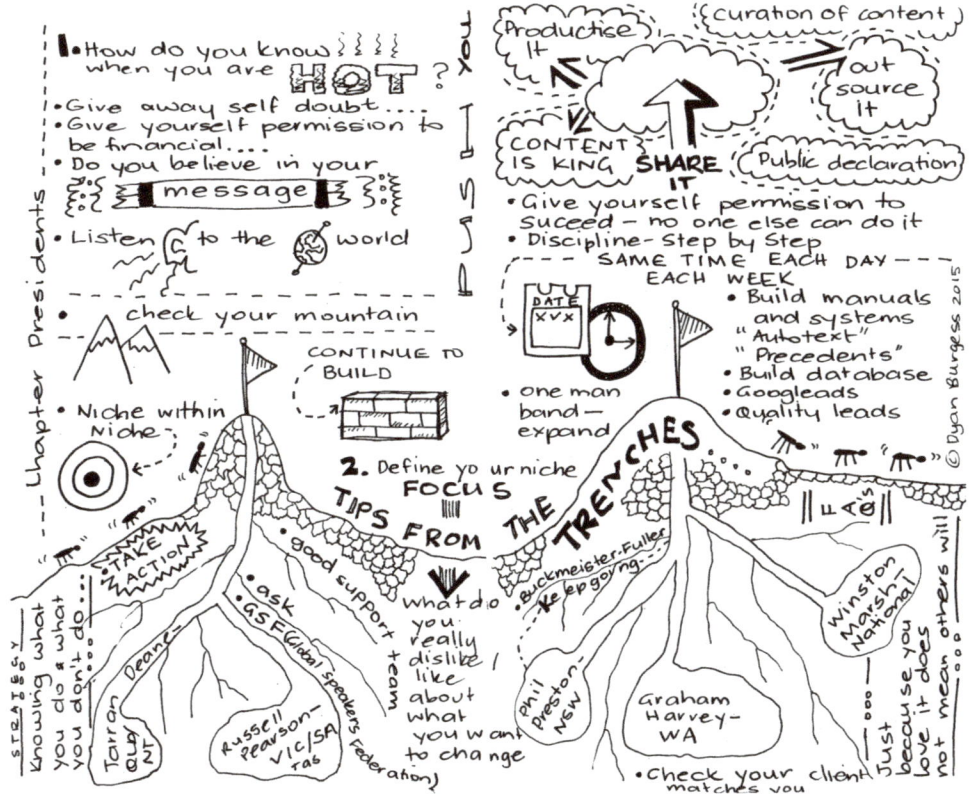

# NATIONAL COUNCIL OF WOMEN QUEENSLAND – PARENTS AND CHILDREN'S CONFERENCE

> ## "I HAVE NEVER LET MY SCHOOLING INTERFERE WITH MY EDUCATION. "
>
> *— Mark Twain*

## Make a Twist • Michele Juratowitch

**NWCQ • Brisbane, 2014**

Michele encourages parents and teachers to 'make a twist' on the current curriculum in order to extend gifted children beyond their usual classroom learning.

The focus is on higher order thinking rather than just more of the same.

# Boring! • Michele Juratowitch

**NWCQ • Brisbane, 2015**

What is the definition of boredom and why do children use this word?

Are they finding the task too easy or are they too confused?

If we understand what the children are actually saying, we can provide sufficient challenge and personal growth.

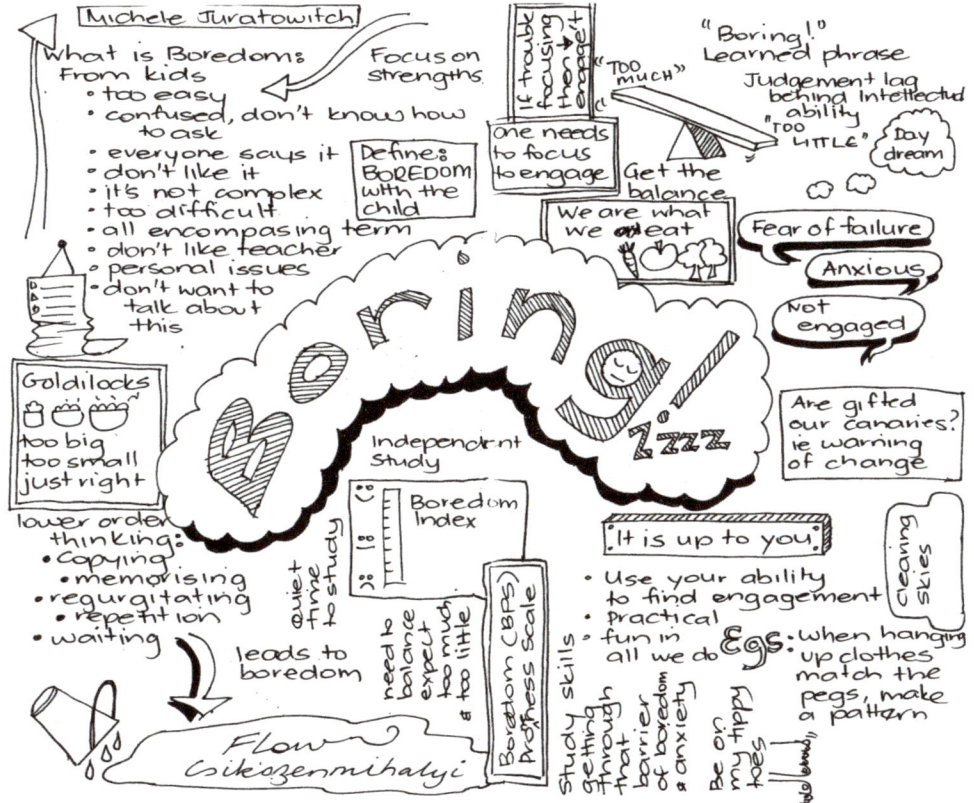

## The Future of Education •
## Gabrielle Austenberry

**NWCQ • Brisbane, 2014**

The Internet of Things (IoT) is here and we need to consider its potential in helping children to learn.

This is already happening with organisations such as Khan Academy and with Sugatra Mutra's School in the Cloud.

How can we best blend traditional learning and digital learning to meet the needs of the next generation?

# The Emotional Needs of Your Child • Mandy Dovey

**NWCQ • Brisbane, 2015**

Having dropped out of guide dog school, George (the dog), is helping school children to build emotional resilience.

Children chat with George, read him books and tell him their problems.

His presence has had an extremely positive effect helping children with day-to-day concerns.

## Attention and Executive Functioning • Dr Fiona Jones, Jordane Bennezz & Rachel D'Amico

**NWCQ • Brisbane, 2015**

Keep it simple, intense and regular in order to stimulate children's minds.

Distracted minds and distracted bodies make it difficult for children to learn.

The most important question about children's behaviour is 'does this affect the ability to live day-to-day?'. If not, don't worry about it; if it does, get an assessment.

ATTENTION EXECUTIVE functioning – Dr Fiona Jones, Jordane Bennett and Rachel D'Amigo. Keep it simple, intense & regular

**OT** = skills for living

BUILDING MOTIVATION
working memory
initiation
monitoring
emotional control
inhibition

true exceptional

SHOW OPTIONS FOR STEPS

Timer

ALERTNESS
↳ Interest
↳ Touch
↳ Movement

OPTIONS
↳ iPad
↳ screen
↳ set goals
↳ self grade success

DISTRACTED MIND

DISTRACTED BODY

work out what needs to support the lack of information. what tools can be used to assist self control

unhardness can hide disability

DOES THIS AFFECT THE ABILITY TO LIVE DAY TO DAY
if not, don't worry, if it does get an assessment

Strategies
• motivation
• cognitive

the disability

Routines Boundaries
HABITS
HABITS
HABITS

• Avoid
• Replace
• Predictability
• self talk

can hide giftedness

disability

• Relatedness
• Competence
• Autonomy

Safe & Secure
HOW WE TAKE IN NEW INFORMATION

Sensory Information
↓  ↓  ↓  ↓  ↓

How this is processed can then provide a physical response

If not enough information received when processing then brain will request more feedback

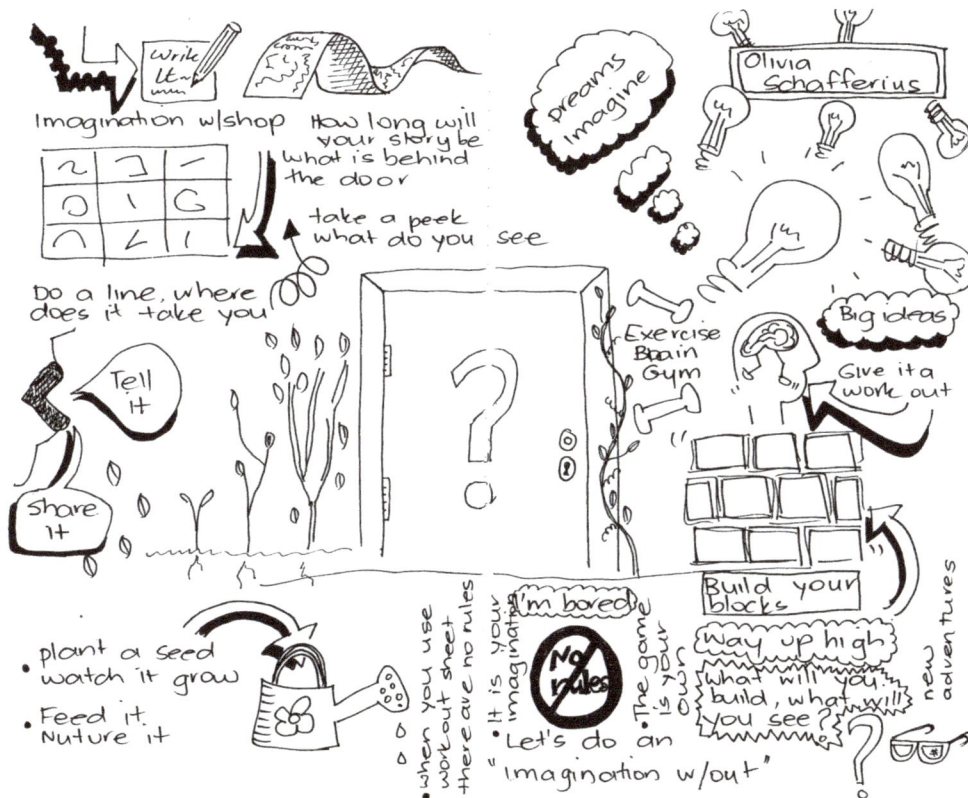

## Imagination Workshop • Olivia Schafferius

**NWCQ • Brisbane , 2014**

Draw a line. Where does it take you?

Using your imagination is like planting a seed and watching it grow.

However, you need to feed it and nurture it if you want it to cultivate big ideas.

# PODCASTS

**"THERE'S NO SHORTAGE OF REMARKABLE IDEAS; WHAT'S MISSING IS THE WILL TO EXECUTE THEM. "**

— *Seth Godin*

### Emma Mactaggart

## How one women's dream became a book collection on Jetstar •

#### Bringing Our Books to You • Podcast • Brisbane 2015

Emma shows the power of a simple conversation with a friend when her Boogie Books became a permanent resident on Jet Star Flights throughout Australia.

Passionate about helping children to publish their own stories, Emma has produced over 400 titles with children under her Boogie Books publishing house.

Emma

≡ MAC TAGG ART ≡ CHILD WRITES ≡

'help children create stories, help children create communities by providing children with publishing platforms.'

www.childwrites.com.au
www.writersweb.com.au

Books by Emma
* Lily Fabourama Glamourama
* I Can Do Anything
* Child writes

Ippy Gold Medal
QPRCWN Strong Women Awards 2012

Scaffold 4 kids
Based in Toowoomba
Childwrites
Founder
Expert Academy 2014
Speakers Ink
writers web

## Inside the mind of a Brilliant Illustrator and Graphic Designer • Christy Martin

**Bringing Our Books to You • Podcast • Brisbane 2015**

Brilliant artist, Christy Martin, shares her techniques for success in illustration and graphic design. She reminisces on how her early childhood opportunities laid the foundations for her life, and talks about how she balances the challenges of motherhood.

# POWER TO TRAIN
# DR RICH ALLEN

# "I FEEL THAT LUCK IS PREPARATION MEETING OPPORTUNITY."

— *Opray Winfrey*

## Training Program • Dr Rich Allen

### Power to Train • Sydney, 2015

Rich reminds us that everything we do has a purpose and encourages us to always keep this at the top of our minds.

DAY 1

The Power to Train

RICH ALLEN

30 NOVEMBER 2015

We are what we constantly do...

REFLECT

Everything we do... HAS A PURPOSE

Good thoughts

Unhappy thoughts

Where are you putting these?

Relatable Context Commonalities

Ask questions...

Open questions

room to grow
understand where you are

Was introduced you yourself

TO CONNECT

Pick your introduction depending on your audience

EXPERT-EASE what you do without thinking

Start here

BEING PRESENT
Getting the most out of this moment...

Start small & expand those (see) what works

Acknowledge IT move on...

If you get a negative comment person opinion

Let it go...

move your body to the side to deflate the negative energy

©Dyan Burgess 2015

# Training Program • Dr Rich Allen

## Power to Train • Sydney, 2015

Rich emphasises the importance of nurturing the process of memory building. His tips include:

(1) use physical actions to support mental memories
(2) provide information in 10-unit bursts
(3) be prepared to be silent.

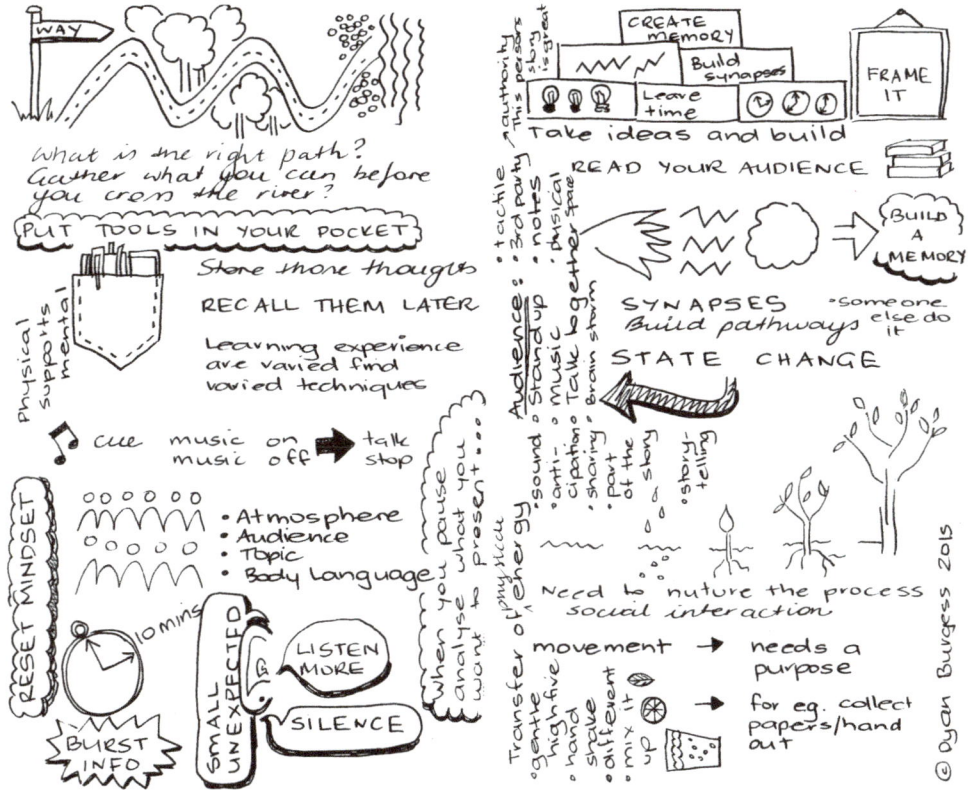

WAY

What is the right path? Gather what you can before you cross the river?

PUT TOOLS IN YOUR POCKET

Store those thoughts

RECALL THEM LATER

Learning experience are varied find varied techniques

Physical supports mental

cue music on music off → talk stop

RESET MINDSET

10 mins

○○○○○○
○○○○○

• Atmosphere
• Audience
• Topic
• Body Language

BURST INFO

SMALL UNEXPECTED

LISTEN MORE

SILENCE

When you pause analyse what you want to present...

CREATE MEMORY
Build synapses
Leave time

story is great
authority
This person

Take ideas and build

FRAME IT

READ YOUR AUDIENCE

BUILD A MEMORY

SYNAPSES
Build pathways
• someone else do it

STATE CHANGE

Audience:
• tactile
• 3rd party
• notes
• physical
• stand up
• music
• anti-cipation
• Talk together
• Brain storm
• sharing
• part of the story
• story-telling

Transfer of physical energy
• gentle
• high five
• hand shake
• mix it up
• different

Need to nuture the process social interaction

movement → needs a purpose

for eg. collect papers/hand out

© Dyan Burgess 2015

## Training Program • Dr Rich Allen

### Power to Train • Sydney, 2015

Rich suggests key points to remember when addressing an audience:

(1) keep the presentation simple and relevant

(2) focus on showing, not telling

(3) weave in a story or two.

TELEVISION EDUCATION NETWORK

**"DO THE BEST YOU CAN UNTIL YOU KNOW BETTER. THEN WHEN YOU KNOW BETTER, DO BETTER."**

— *Maya Angelou*

## Estate Planning and Division 7A •
## Damian O'Connor

**TEN Conference • Gold Coast, 2015**

Legal advice is important when it comes to estate planning and Division 7A .

Advisers need to understand the tax determinations and case studies to ensure that individual circumstances are considered correctly.

## Family Trusts and the Blended Family • Matthew Burgess

**TEN Conference • Gold Coast, 2015**

Matthew outlines the 101 trust principles and the basic makeup of what constitutes a trust.

To ensure you are providing accurate advice, he suggests using checklists and keeping up to date with current case law around trusts.

## I was Depending on You • John Armfield

**TEN Conference • Gold Coast, 2015**

John provides a definition of family provision claims. He then discusses the complications that can occur and how the scenarios might be resolved.

Ultimately, claims need to be based on best practice practical outcomes, as well as knowing how much and what assets are available under the estate.

JOHN ARMFIELD – I WAS DEPENDING ON U

Preparedness is vital to set goals for mediation

**1** Family Provision Claims – what are they?

- Eligible Applicants
- Different rules each state and territory
- Statutory exception to the general law principle – testator free to leave to whom they please
- Court given DISCRETIONARY power to INTERFERE

Vigolo v Bostin (2005) 221 CLR 191 per Gleeson CJ

**2** Former/De Facto Spouse

- Each state
  - check the law of the jurisdiction
- One thing to be eligible – but what does that mean
- Will they be successful?
- What are consequences?
- Claim
  - ? existent
  - non-existent
  - not strong
- How long ago?

PRECEDENTS/TEMPLATES

Grandchildren Step Kids Foster children

**3** Timing

- What is the time frame that needs to be met?
- How will this effect the estate?
- What are current rulings around these timings?
- Check law of your state or territory
- Each state or territory own rules

where are U

TAX IMPLICATIONS

**4** Is there enough MONEY?

- Is it worth it
- What are the options
- Nothing of Nothing is still Nothing

REVERSE RESPONDER

Marshall vs Carruthers

- Limited funds
  BEST PRACTICE
- How much? What assets?

FEE SIMPLE INTEREST s.t. A CHARGE © 2015 Dyan Burgess

## Aged Care and the New Partner Dilemma • Brian Herd

**TEN Conference • Gold Coast, 2015**

Elder Law is here and now, and is becoming increasingly complex with the range of relationships that exist in this space.

It's important to seek financial advice for any family members approaching or in aged care.

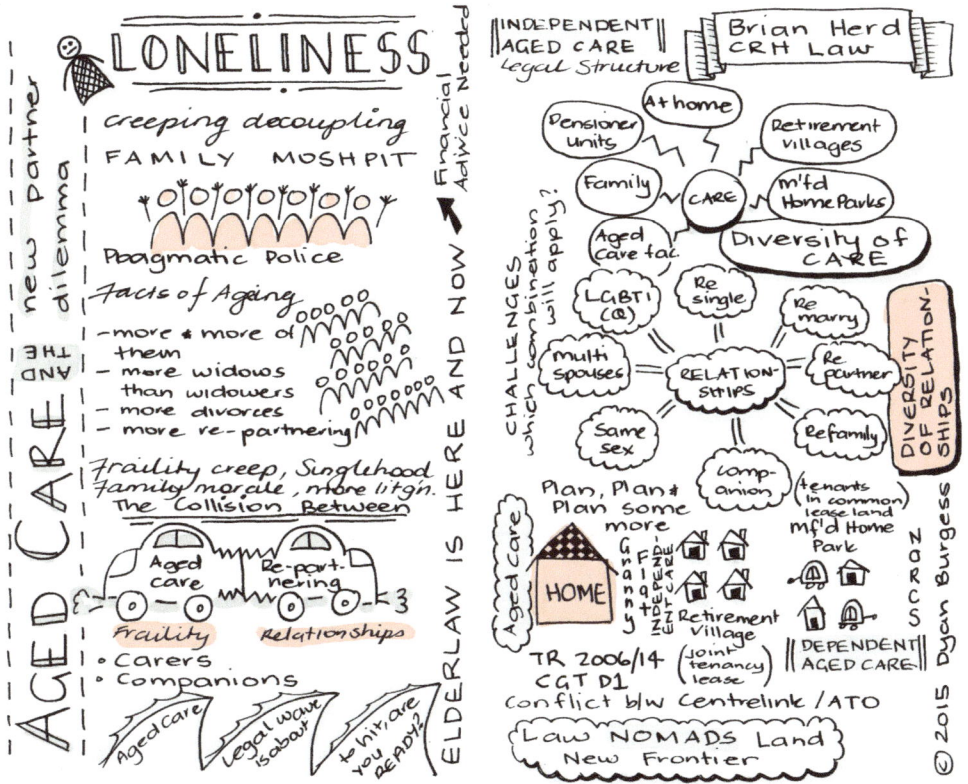

## Blended Family Dynamics as they Effect the Estate Plan • Craig Spink

**TEN Conference • Gold Coast, 2015**

Estate planning for blended families needs to be considered on a case-by-case basis. It is important to understand the individual circumstances to provide the best advice to clients.

The challenge is to tailor a plan that will look at what the client has presented as well as the attitude of the individuals involved.

## Vesting Dates • Matthew Burgess

**TEN Conference • Gold Coast, 2015**

Ultimately, 'it depends'; each scenario needs to be carefully reviewed to understand the exact facts of the case. However, the starting point is always to read the deed.

Once facts are known, we can start to understand the implications of each of the scenarios and their legal and tax consequences.

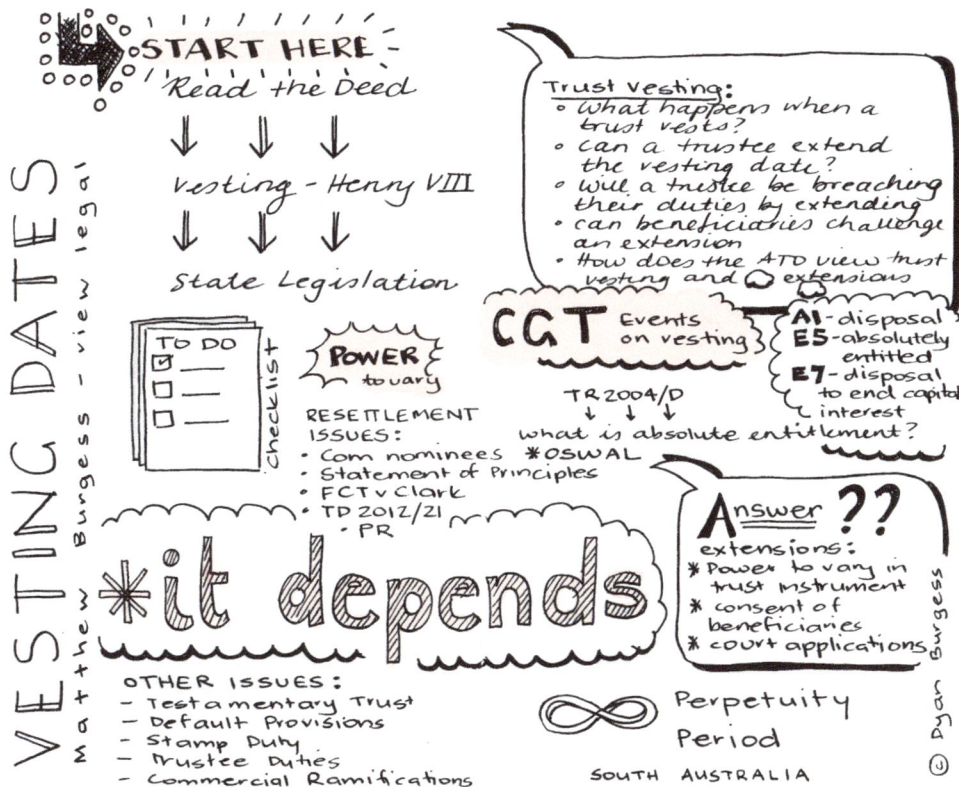

## Common Issues of Testamentary Trusts • Hall & Wilcox Lawyers

**TEN Conference • Gold Coast, 2015**

When it comes to testamentary trusts the ultimate question is, *what did the will maker intend?*

If there is an issue with a trust deed, can the will maker's intentions be successfully followed?

What are the costs to enable the best outcome for all parties?

Advisors need to look closely at practical issues and solutions.

## Getting Old: Ensuring the estate plan does not ossify as well • Brian Herd

**TEN Conference • Gold Coast, 2015**

According to Brian, the 'new old' is sun-baked, well cooked, tattooed and body pierced. And their relationships come in all shapes and sizes, not always fitting neatly into existing laws.

With an increase in village romance, including de factos and 'compactos' (where couples spend a lot of time together but don't actually live together), he encourages all parties to plan carefully and understand the laws.

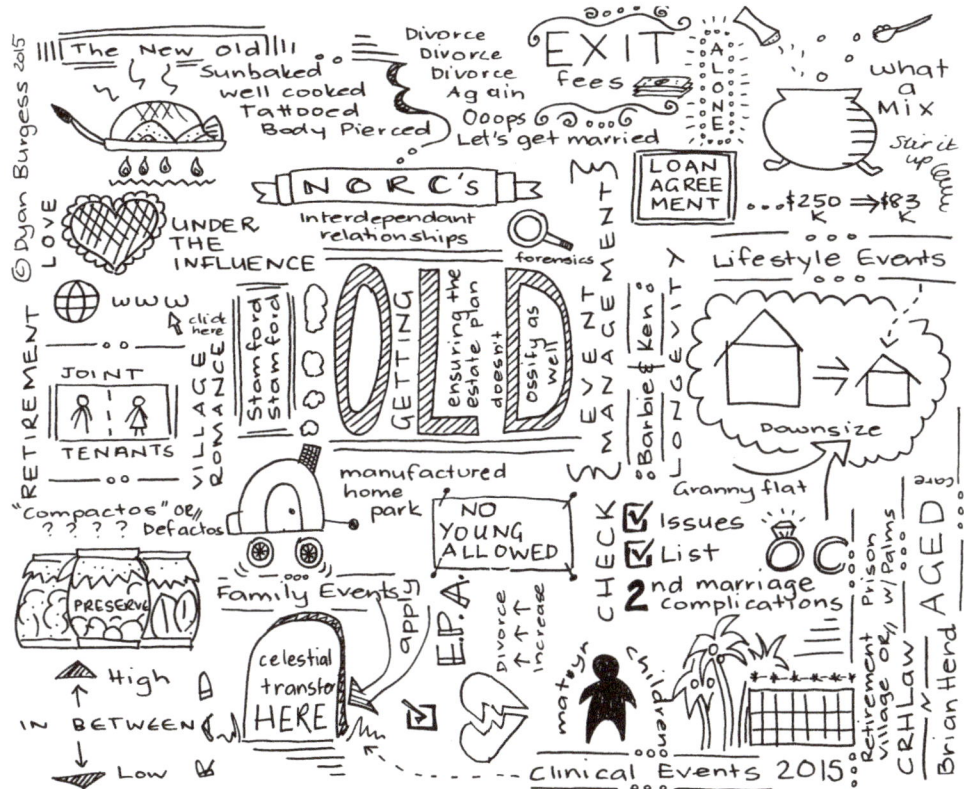

## Using Post-Death Testamentary Trusts to Fix Estate Planning Problems • Matthew Burgess

**TEN Conference • Gold Coast, 2015**

Of course, doing it right the first time is the best option. However, this is not always the reality.

While post-death testamentary trusts are a reactive strategy, they can ultimately get the intended result.

But, most likely, you will need to have a compromise checklist.

# ULTIMATE BUSINESS PROPELLOR

"**FEARLESSNESS IS LIKE A MUSCLE. I KNOW FROM MY OWN LIFE THAT THE MORE THAT I EXERCISE IT THE MORE NATURAL IT BECOMES TO NOT LET MY FEARS RUN ME.**"

— *Arianna Huffington*

## Ultimate Business Propellor Workshop • Lauren Clemett

**Brisbane, 2015**

Lauren reminds us that we need to be our own Personal Branding Consultancy.

Learn how to package 'you', clearly articulate your 'why' and 'what', and be consistent with your brand.

## Ultimate Business Propellor Workshop • Lauren Clemett

### Brisbane , 2015

Lauren encourages us to get inside the consumer brain.

By doing so we can start to ask what the consumer needs, what they are interested in, and why they would pay for our services.

Once we have answers to these questions, we will have a better idea of how to make our service visible.

## Ultimate Business Propeller Workshop • Lauren Clemett

**Brisbane , 2015**

'Know your why' was central to Lauren's talk.

She reminds us that the confused brain will never buy anything.

Her advice is to use our stories, our passion and our authentic selves to build our brand.

## Ultimate Business Propeller Workshop • Lauren Clemett

**Brisbane , 2015**

Lauren urges us to ask ourselves a few questions:

(1)  what do I want to be paid for?
(2)  what is it that people will say about me?
(3)  what do I want to be known for?
(4)  what am I at my best doing?

You need to become that specialist; use your experience to become a niche within a niche.

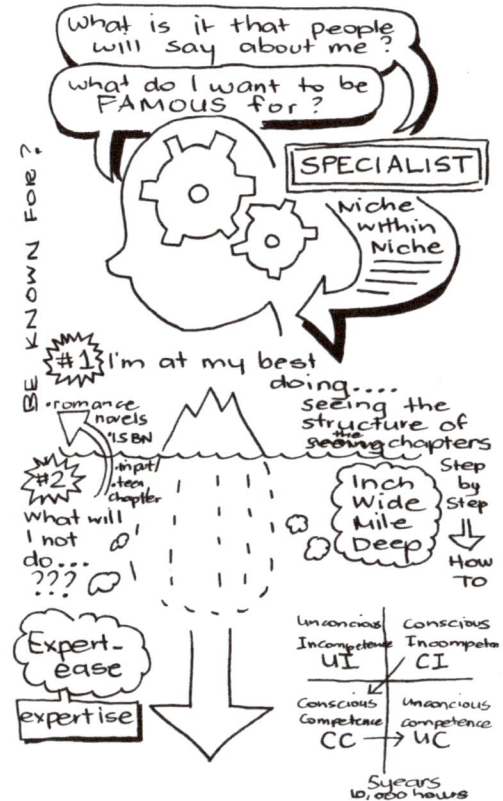

# WEBINARS

> **"LIFE-FULFILLING WORK IS NEVER ABOUT THE MONEY — WHEN YOU FEEL TRUE PASSION FOR SOMETHING, YOU INSTINCTIVELY IND WAYS TO NUTURE IT."**
>
> — *Eileen Fisher*

## Seven-Figure Business Coaching
### • Taki Moore & Rob Nixon

**Black Belt Master Class • Webinar, June 2015**

Taki and Rob discuss the use of a Score Board to help achieve goals in a seven-figure business. Participants need to be held accountable for the promises made to themselves. Keeping those promises sees success for the business; not keeping those promises will almost certainly guarantee failure.

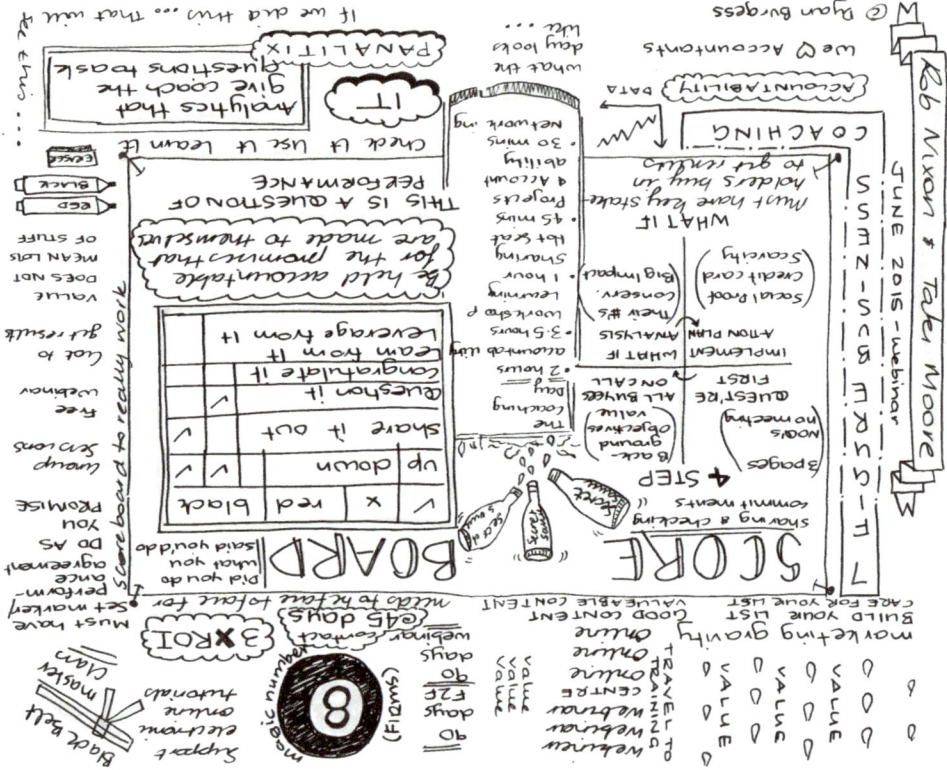

# Bernard Salt • Infographic Speaking Circuit

**LinkedIn Pulse Letter, 2015**

This is my interpretation of an existing infographic about Bernard Salt.

I mean, with a surname like Salt, how could I resist creating my own salt trail to represent his talks over the course of a year?

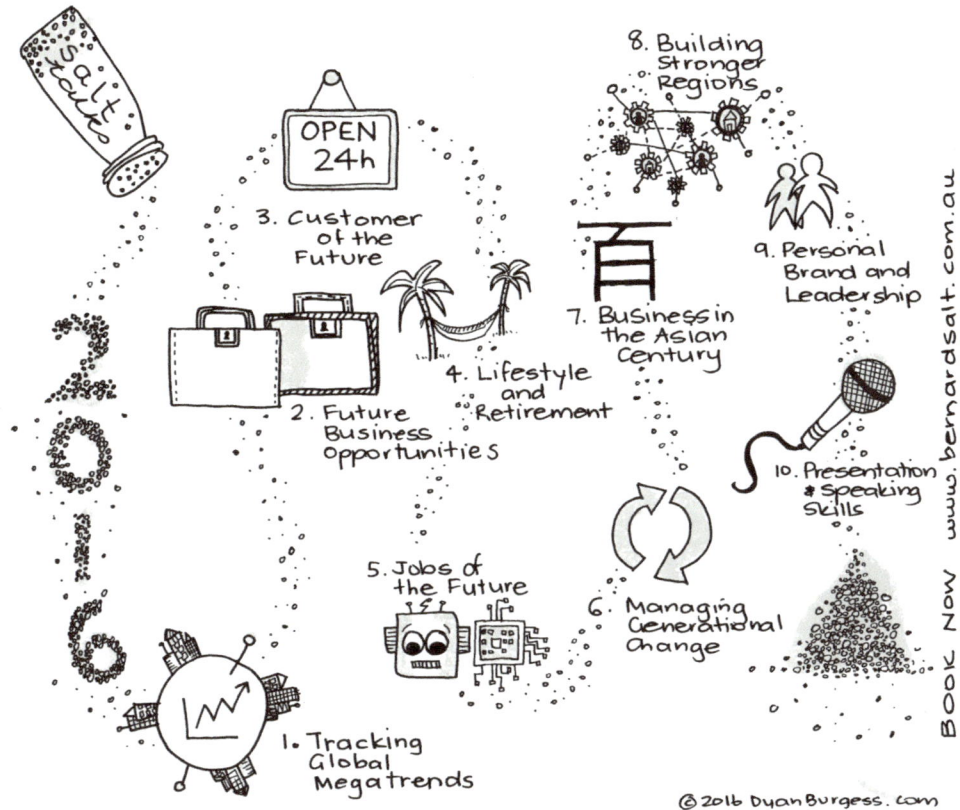

3. Customer of the Future

2. Future Business Opportunities

4. Lifestyle and Retirement

5. Jobs of the Future

6. Managing Generational Change

7. Business in the Asian Century

8. Building Stronger Regions

9. Personal Brand and Leadership

10. Presentation & Speaking Skills

1. Tracking Global Megatrends

www.bernardsalt.com.au

Book Now

© 2016 DyanBurgess.com

# WOMEN IN THOUGHT LEADERSHIP

**"I ATTRIBUTE MY SUCCESS TO THIS; I NEVER GAVE OR TOOK ANY EXCUSE. "**

— *Florence Nightingale*

## Conscious Capitalism • Professor Judith McLean and Olivia's Lunch • Maria Clark

**Women in Leadership • Brisbane, 2015**

Conscious capitalism: how can and should those with wealth share their good fortune with others?

Olivia's Lunch is Maria Clark's story of how she created a foundation based on her experiences with premature babies. Via an annual luncheon, she has raised over $300,000 for the Mater Critical Care Unit in Brisbane.

## MindPT Founder • Kim Serafini and Cherish Foundation • Professor Andreas Obermoir

**Women in Leadership • Brisbane, 2015**

Kim is the creator of the MindPT app, which is revolutionising the way we think, live, learn and love. Based on science, the app rebuilds neural pathways to practically implement the theory of positive psychology.

The Cherish Foundation seeks to find kinder ways to treat women in relation to genealogical treatment, particularly cancer.

**LeadX • Kristine Carlson • Megan Houghton • Sonia McDonald • Monica Bradley • Annette Sym • Mary Jane Bellotti • Dr Kirsten Baulch • Kim Serafini**

**Women in Leadership • Brisbane, 2015**

Leading women entrepreneurs discuss innovation in their specific industries.

In particular, they highlight the role of technology in improving businesses, and the need to innovate in order to create better outcomes for clients.

## Katie Noonan and Precious Wings • Kerry Gordon & Kristie Shaw

### Women in Leadership • Brisbane, 2015

Katie spoke about being a women entrepreneur in the music industry and how 'a series of happy accidents' created her path to where she is today.

Precious Wings allows families and friends to find the first steps to assist in copying with the loss of a child.

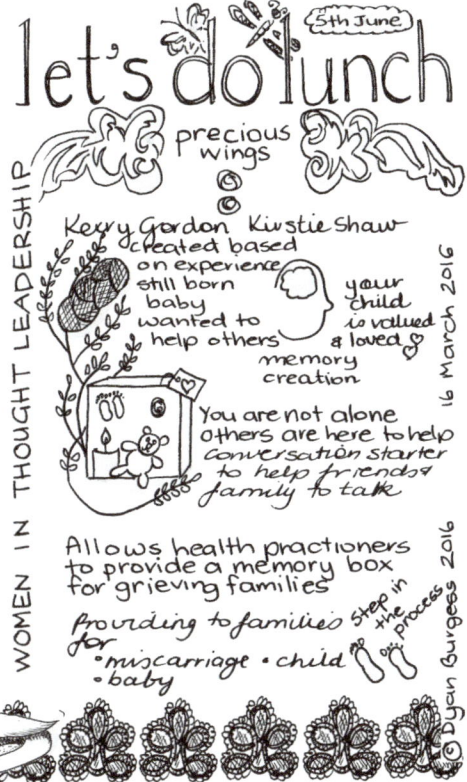

> ## "DON'T BE INTIMIDATED BY WHAT YOU DON'T KNOW. THAT CAN BE YOUR GREATEST STRENGTH AND ENSURE THAT YOU DO THINGS DIFFERENTLY FROM EVERYONE ELSE. "
>
> — *Sara Blakely*

# Final Word of Thanks

Thank you for reading to my final page.

I hope that it is your beginning page; may you create wonderful visual notes to assist with your life learning.

# Other Books By Dyan Burgess

How to Bake a Business Book

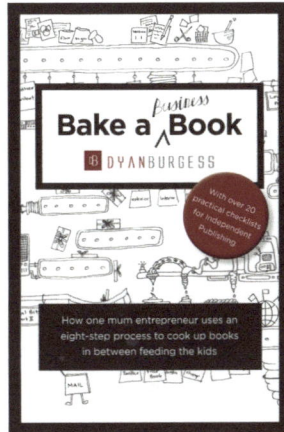

Wanting to publish a book about your expertise? Thought that you don't have the time or the content.

Wanting a business card that has more than your name and email address on it?

What if you handed prospects a book that you published? Would that make a difference to your business?

This book provides an entrepreneur mum's eight-step process to cook up independently published business books in between feeding four kids.

## D. I. Y. Tangled Patterns

Want to draw like a tangle artist? Not sure that you can, or don't think you have the time.

Want to give personalised art to your family and friends but not sure how?

This book provides examples and practice space for you to create your own personalised colouring images.

By spending those 'in-between' minutes using this practical book, you can build your own beautiful patterns and build great relaxing skills.

Relax. Breathe. Draw. Enjoy.

# Further Reading

Interested in learning more about visual note taking?

(1) Mike Rohde's books, *The Sketchnote Handbook* and *The Sketchnote Workbook*, are wonderful resources for building your skills.

(2) Lynne Cazaly's books, *Create Change* and *Visual Mojo*, will also help build your drawing skills.

(3) Guy Downes (www.guydownes.com) has been in the industry for over a decade in Australia.

(4) *Think in Colour* (www.think-in-colour.com.au) is the brainchild of Jessamy Gee and provides a bright and vibrant summary of concepts.

# Acknowledgement

Thank you to the people who have kept me on track:

My family – immediate, extended and in-laws

Virtualplicity

Dedicated Book Designs

Each time I read a book I take a little bit away and store it in my mind for later retrieval. All that storing has come together in this book.

Thank you to those who have chosen to share their stories in print so that I can learn from you.

"We are what we repeatedly do" – Aristotle

# About the Author

Dyan is passionate about helping entrepreneurs to convert their valuable experiences into compelling, multi-platform, independently published books or visual notes (for those looking for a quick solution)

In her work as Creative Director for *Words From Daddy's Mouth*, she knows first-hand what it is like to pull the best bits of many and varied experiences into unique and passionate stories.

As a country girl beginning life in rural Victoria and NSW, you can imagine the gorgeous surrounds, quirky people and outdoor adventures that dotted the landscape of her early years. A fascination with people and their vast potential followed her through a science degree in Brisbane, Australia, extending into two decades of banking and finance, travel adventures, family creation and business development.

Understanding the multiple facets of processes has always been incredibly fascinating to Dyan. However, to writers (and entrepreneurs), understanding your internal step-by-step guide can sometimes seem redundant (and boring) – and can be a barrier to publishing great ideas.

Fortunately, Dyan enjoys collaboration. So whether you are interested in the technical aspects of publishing, or you simply want to create a visual note or write a book on your expertise (and avoid the boring bits), she can work with you to achieve your dreams.

**Simply put – Getting it Done.**

National Library of Australia Cataloguing-in-Publication entry

**Creator:**  Burgess, Dyan, author and illustrator.

**Title:**  Title: The Visual Note Taking Handbook: using visual notes to get more out of lectures, lessons, presentations and books / Dyan Burgess.

**ISBN:**  978-1-925406-25-2 (paperback)

**ISBN:**  978-1-925406-26-9 (ebook : Kindle)

**ISBN:**  978-1-925406-27-6 (ebook : epub)

**Subjects:**  Note-taking—Drawings.
Study skills—Handbooks, manuals, etc.
Visual learning.

**Other Creators/Contributors:**  Dedicated Book Services, (www.netdbs.com).

**Dewey Number:**  371.30281

When reviewing could you please reference my website www.dyanburgess.com.

While the author has made every effort to provide accurate Internet addresses at the time of publication, neither the author nor the publisher assumes responsibility for errors, or changes that occur after publication. Further the publisher does not have any control over and does not assume any responsibility for author or third-party websites or their content.

Published by D & M Fancy Pastry Pty Ltd in 2016

www.ingramcontent.com/pod-product-compliance
Lightning Source LLC
Chambersburg PA
CBHW041228270326
41935CB00006B/58